Churches
IN BRISTOL

by

Bryan Little

one of a series of booklets
published for the City of Bristol

by

THE REDCLIFFE PRESS

First published in 1978 by
REDCLIFFE PRESS LTD
14 Dowry Square, Bristol 8

A083703

© Bryan Little

Printed in Great Britain by
BURLEIGH LTD
Bristol

ISBN 0 905459 06 7

CONTENTS

In the text, each church is numbered as above, and the locations of all **except** those asterisked* are marked on the map on the inside rear cover.

St. James': west front

Below Bristol Cathedral (St. Augustine's Abbey) from the south east

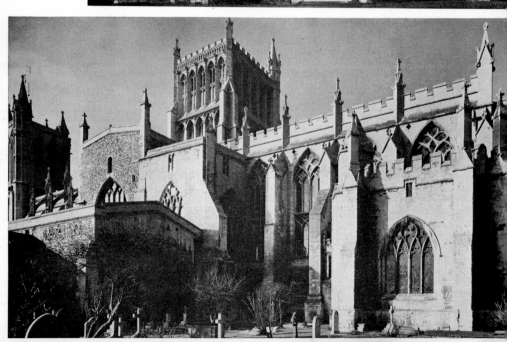

INTRODUCTION

Few cities in England can equal Bristol in the number and quality of its ancient churches. Nor is Bristol to be disregarded for the merits of its more recent places of worship. The sheer size of London, or of such provincial cities as Birmingham and Manchester, means that they have more Victorian and post-Victorian churches than a West Country city whose people number fewer than half a million. But Bristol's modern places of worship, one of them by wide consent a supreme example of the church architecture completed, in this country, within the last ten years, should be neglected neither by the city's own people nor by visitors and tourists.

The reasons for Bristol's great wealth of 'historic' church architecture are easy to understand. Like Bruges or Antwerp, or Genoa or Venice, Bristol was, in the Middle Ages, an important centre of trade and commerce and, by English medieval standards, a populous place. It was therefore well filled, before the Reformation, with parish churches or with the churches of religious houses. Though it was not, before Henry VIII's reign, the seat of a bishopric it had an important abbey and establishments of all the four main orders of friars. Some of its adjacent villages, now within the boundaries of an expanded city, also have old churches of more than average interest.

In the post-Reformation centuries Bristol never, before the bombings of 1940 and 1941, had any disaster like that of the Great Fire which in 1666 destroyed most of London's medieval churches. But it was, during much of the eighteenth century, England's second city—a wealthy place with enough money wholly or partly to rebuild some of its medieval churches and, before the end of the Georgian age, to erect some wholly new places of worship. This process was not confined to the Church of England. The Nonconformists, including the Quakers and the Unitarians, shared in the city's prosperity; they built many important chapels, a few of which still stand in or near the city's historic centre. By the beginning of the Victorian period—itself by no means without its triumphs in the field of church architecture—Bristol was secure in its position, since maintained despite bombings and other losses, as one of England's best places for a visit by anyone who loves and venerates beautiful places of worship.

5

For some centuries after Bristol's foundation, at an unknown date in the Anglo-Saxon period, the whole town lay on the northern, or Gloucestershire, side of the river whose bridge gave the town its name. The town, like most of the rest of Gloucestershire, was in the diocese of Worcester. Two of the churches, St. Peter's and SS. Philip and James the Less, had mainly urban congregations but also had parishes which stretched well out into the countryside east of the town. Most of the other parish churches in the original, and eventually expanded town north of Bristol Bridge were typical of those of such other medieval English towns as York, London, or Norwich. They were numerous and they had small parishes, and in some cases very few parishioners. Some of their buildings were correspondingly small, and only one, St. Stephen's, exceeded what the inhabitants of such a town would have considered a moderate size. But in their architectural quality, and in the beauty of their contents they were, and largely still are, of the utmost merit. They have been diminished by the demolition of four churches (St. Lawrence's, St. Leonard's, St. Ewen's and St. Werburgh's) and by the bombing, without any rebuilding, of St. Peter's and St. Mary-le-Port. But those which remain are immensely worth seeing.

Bristol's chief religious houses, and three of the medieval town's four friaries, were also north of the Avon and also on the side away from the town's smaller river the Frome. In the siting of their monasteries or friaries their founders followed a normal practice whereby such establishments, with the extensive buildings needed by their occupants, had to be started on open and spacious sites outside the town boundaries. The largest, though not the earliest, of these religious houses was St. Augustine's Abbey of Augustinian canons regular. The eastern part of its church remains as part of the most important of the city's places of worship.

Bristol Cathedral[1]

Bristol is unique among England's larger commercial and industrial cities in having a mainly medieval cathedral of the cruciform shape and size (over three hundred feet long) which Englishmen associate with a cathedral. Other great cities, Birmingham or Liverpool or Sheffield, have as their Anglican cathedrals modern buildings or parish churches converted and enlarged. Bristol Cathedral, like the city, is rooted in a prosperous medieval past.

St. Augustine's Abbey was founded in the 1140s; the canons used the church and the domestic buildings till the abbey's dissolution in 1539. The nave, perhaps largely ruinous, was then destroyed, but in 1542 the rest of the church became the cathedral of Henry VIII's new Bristol bishopric. In 1836 this was merged with that of Gloucester, but Bristol Cathedral kept its status, and its nave, anticipating a restored bishopric, was built in the Victorian period. Since 1897 the enlarged cathedral has been the mother church of a revived Anglican diocese.

Westbury-on-
Trym
Below St.
Nicholas':
the crypt

The Cathedral
choir: vaulting
in the south
aisle

Norman masonry remains in the South transept, but more spectacular Norman work, perhaps of about 1155, is in the splendid vaulted Chapter House (England's finest chapter house of this period), in its vaulted vestibule with early pointed arches, and in the lowermost storey of the great gateway. Off the North transept the Elder Lady Chapel is a beautiful Early English building of the thirteenth century; it has lancets, rich wall arcading, and delicate carving probably by sculptors who worked, about 1230, at Wells Cathedral.

The architectural glory of Bristol Cathedral lies in the eastern limb which contains the choir and its aisles and a beautiful eastern Lady Chapel. A splendid, pioneering work of the first thirty years after 1300, it has features which anticipated the Perpendicular style. It makes Bristol Cathedral unique, among England's 'greater' churches, in that it was designed, like 'hall churches' on the Continent, with aisles as high as the central space; the aisle vaults required by such a design are rare and ingenious. Its set of tomb recesses, half octagons at the top and with surrounding star pattern decoration, are another great rarity and could have influenced late Gothic work in Spain and Portugal.

The central tower, much restored in the 1890s, is Perpendicular work of about 1470, while the transepts were richly vaulted a little later. The nave by G. E. Street, of 1867–77 and with its western towers finished by 1888, is an important piece of Victorian church architecture, modelled on the earlier choir but with some distinctive features of Street's devising.

Bristol Cathedral is important for its late Saxon sculpture showing Christ harrowing hell, for medieval effigies of Berkeleys, and for particularly fine effigies of late medieval abbots. The Elizabethan, seventeenth century and Georgian monuments are also notable. The Cathedral has some pre-Reformation screen and stall work, and a splendid Baroque organ case of about 1685. Some of its glass is of about 1330, while other old glass, in a more fragmentary state, is late medieval. One window has important glazing of the 1660s. Two special treasures are the late medieval brass chandelier (the finest in England) once in the bombed Temple Church, and the two silver candlesticks, of 1712, given by a promoter of the privateering voyage under Woodes Rogers who rescued Alexander Selkirk and thus gave Defoe much material for *Robinson Crusoe*.

The Lord Mayor's Chapel (St. Mark's)[2]

This is one of the very few churches in England owned and maintained by a municipality. It was originally the church of the Hospital, or charitable institution, of St. Mark, founded in the thirteenth century by Sir Maurice de Gaunt (a kinsman of the Berkeleys) and his nephew Robert de Gournay. The hospital was dissolved when the monasteries were suppressed, and the church was then acquired by the Corporation. Among various uses it has served as the chapel of Queen Elizabeth's Hospital School.

The long, narrow building is partly of the thirteenth century, with a side chapel of about 1320. The tower dates from 1487, and the East end of the church was splendidly reconstructed about 1520, which is also the approximate date of the beautiful little Poyntz chantry, fan-vaulted and with its floor laid with coloured Spanish tiles of the same period. Another side chapel is also of the early sixteenth century. The North transept is a late Victorian rebuild.

The contents of this beautiful church are so splendid and varied that they cannot here be fully described. There are chain-mailed effigies of the founders and some beautiful late medieval tombs, including one of a bishop of Llandaff, and a splendid range of post-Reformation monuments of various dates. Magnificent Baroque ironwork by William Edney, the famous Bristol smith, has been moved in from the bombed Temple Church. The glass in some of the windows is of special note. Some of it, particularly the heraldic and other glass grouped in the East window, was always in St. Mark's, but much of the rest is magnificent glass of the Renaissance period, originally in France and other Continental countries, which was once in private collections but which was bought, in the 1820s, by the Bristol Corporation. Some of the best was in William Beckford's great collection at Fonthill 'Abbey'. This church is closed on Fridays and in August.

St. James' Priory[3]

Often said to be the oldest city church, St. James' has certainly retained a larger part of its Norman fabric than any other Bristol church. The priory, comparatively small and a 'cell' or dependency of the great Benedictine abbey at Tewkesbury, was founded about 1120 by Robert, Earl of Gloucester, the most powerful and important of Henry I's bastard sons. When the earl died in 1148 he was buried in the eastern part of the church; this was gradually destroyed after the dissolution.

The present church consists of the five western bays of the priory's Norman nave, a modest structure compared with the churches of great abbeys like Tewkesbury, and with no triforium gallery between its arches and the upper row of clerestory windows. It is, however, of considerable dignity, and its western façade is of great architectual importance for its row of intersecting arches and the rare interlaced design of its much worn wheel window.

The western part of the nave became a parish church in 1374 (hence its survival after the dissolution), and the much restored tower, of early Perpendicular architecture, was then built to hold the parish bells; the fine timber roof with its stone corbels, now brightly painted, are of the same period. The South aisle was widened late in the seventeenth century, but the inner North aisle, which adjoined the monks' cloisters, is of the original Norman width.

The church, whose parish was one of the most populous in old Bristol, has many monuments to important parishioners, among them Sir James Russell, a former Governor of Nevis in the West Indies, who died in 1674.

Four towers:

Left St. John the Baptist,

Right St. Stephen's,

Below left Temple,

Below right Brislington

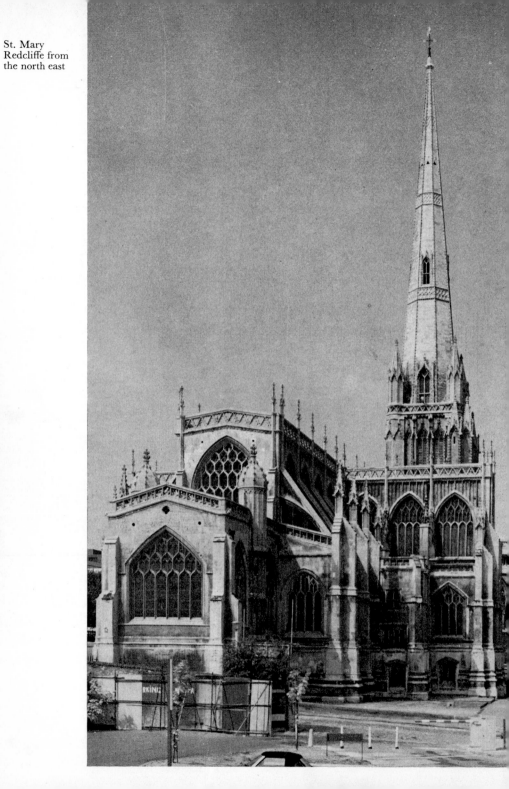

St. Mary
Redcliffe from
the north east

More important, under an arch of the thirteenth century, is the beautiful effigy, of about 1230, showing a man in civilian costume; it seems likely to be by one of the school of sculptors who worked on the West end of Wells Cathedral.

St. Peter's and St. Mary-le-Port[4, 5]

These historic churches—perhaps the earliest, by foundation, in the city centre—were gutted by wartime bombing, and the remains of both are now preserved by the City.

St. Peter's, built at the townward end of what was once a large rural parish, may occupy the site first used in the town of Bristol for any religious building. The lower part of its tower is simple Norman work, and its North aisle seems always to have had its narrow Norman dimensions. But the rest of the church was rebuilt and expanded, probably about 1400, in the early Perpendicular style, so that the windows and the surviving parts of the pillars and arches are of that period, as also is the top stage of the tower. A fine late seventeenth-century altarpiece, and some important monuments, were unhappily lost when the church was bombed. The ruins, in an attractive garden setting, are now an important feature of central Bristol's urban park.

As it stood when it was bombed St. Mary-le-Port was a late medieval church, though it had, in its chancel, some work of the thirteenth century. But post-war excavation proved that a Norman church, perhaps with a Saxon predecessor, had stood on the site. Nothing now remains but the attractive western tower, Perpendicular work of the fifteenth century, and typical of the Bristol area in that the pinnacle above the stairway turret rises high above the other three.

All Saints' (City)[6]

All Saints' is another of the four churches whose small parishes stood close to the central crossroads of the town north of the Avon. Its nave is unusually interesting: its western half is still Norman because buildings were erected over the western end of each aisle before the fifteenth century, while the eastern part of the nave is graceful Perpendicular work, probably of the early fifteenth century, and like other church buildings in Bristol at that time without a clerestory. The chancel is largely modern, but the tower, unusually sited at the north-east corner of the nave, is early Georgian with a charming cupola remodelled in 1807.

The church has the arms of Charles II, a communion table of the late seventeenth century, and several important monuments of local citizens. Of these the finest is that to the well known merchant and philanthropist, Edward Colston. Its Ionic architectural composition is by the famous Georgian architect James Gibbs, while the reclining figure is by the brilliant Flemish immigrant sculptor Rysbrack. It was erected in 1729.

13

All Saints' church has now been adapted for use as an Institute of Christian and Urban Studies.

Christ Church (City) [7]

This stands on the site of a medieval church, and contains several items reinstated from the older building—notably the picturesque quarter jacks of about 1740, the seventeenth-century iron sword rest, the banner of the Bristol Company of Merchant Tailors, and the fine Baroque organ case, of Queen Anne's time, which is now in a Victorian west gallery.

The church itself, built in Bristol's prosperous eighteenth century, replaced the old building in 1786–91 and is a beautiful classical building, with graceful Corinthian columns inside. It has no side galleries, but its general design, by the local architect William Paty, shows the influence of Gibbs' famous church of St. Martin's-in-the-Fields. The same influence also appears in the classical tower, whose graceful spire is capped by a dragon weathervane. The furnishings of the church have been much altered, but the splendid late Georgian altarpiece has been reinstated as a screen, while the beautiful semi-circular communion table, behind altar rails of the same shape, is one of England's finest of its date. The mahogany font is also worth noting; the other font, like a few of the monuments, came from the destroyed church of St. Ewen.

St. John the Baptist [8]

St. John's was one of the four Bristol churches built on stretches of the early medieval town wall after this had ceased to be tactically significant. The gates were still, however, important as barriers, so that the tower and spire of St. John's still rise above the picturesque feature of a vaulted gateway which retains its portcullis groove. The two side entrances are of the early nineteenth century, and the seventeenth-century coats of arms are those of Charles II, the City of Bristol, and the Bristol Merchant Venturers. The tower was originally shared with the small church of St. Lawrence which was pulled down in Elizabeth I's reign and which, on a site immediately to the West, also lay on part of the town wall.

The unaisled church, over the rare feature of a rib-vaulted crypt which may be of two dates, is mostly an excellent early Perpendicular building of about 1380, unusual in its possession of a one-bay upper window designed to give extra light to the rood screen. The beautiful interior has several fine fittings, and the tomb of the church's builder, the rich merchant Walter Frampton (d. 1388) whose civilian effigy is among the finest of its type in England. The church has an excellent Jacobean font, a western gallery with Georgian paintings, a splendid communion table of 1635, an hour glass on the pulpit, and a mural monument by Rysbrack.

St. Stephen's [9]

St. Stephen's church existed in the thirteenth century, and the lower part of its north aisle wall is of the fourteenth century, with two important recessed tombs and civilian effigies of that period. But most of the fabric is Perpendicular Gothic of about 1470, when the church was rebuilt at the expense, largely, of the important merchant family of the Shipwards. It is a typical late medieval town church of considerable size, with no chancel arch, and its clerestory is an unusual feature among Bristol's Perpendicular parish churches. At its south-western corner it has a particularly splendid tower which John Ruskin much admired. Its richly traceried pinnacles in some ways resemble those at Gloucester Cathedral and Dundry, and they have been faithfully renewed and restored at various times. The beautiful South porch has fan vaulting over most of its ceiling.

St. Stephen's, with its special associations with the Merchant Venturers whose bombed hall was in its parish, has a fine range of post-Reformation monuments. The most historic of these is to the seaman Martin Pring (d. 1626) who in 1603 made a pioneering voyage to what later became colonial New England. Splendid Baroque ironwork by Edney, originally in St. Nicholas' and damaged when that church was bombed, was repaired and put in St. Stephen's which also has a medieval brass eagle lectern.

St. Michael's[10]
Often known as St. Michael's-on-the-Mount-Without this church is picturesquely sited on the slope of the hill to which it gives its name—not at the top, but on the skyline as one looks up from the middle of the city. By 1775 the medieval building was in serious disrepair, so it was pulled down and in two years replaced by the present nave and chancel; the attractive fifteenth-century tower, of typically local character, was allowed to remain. The architect was Thomas Paty; his church, Georgian Gothic as it appears from outside, has classical columns in a dignified interior.

SS. Philip and Jacob (James the Less)[11]
The parish served by this church once stretched well into the countryside East of Bristol, and the churchyard still has a rural spaciousness lacking in the churches in the city centre.

As it now stands the church is chiefly medieval, but its nave has been much altered. Originally it was cruciform, and mainly of the early years of the thirteenth century. Its South transept is still in the form of a fine Early English tower, once vaulted and with arches and windows, some of them without capitals, recalling contemporary work at Wells Cathedral; an arch of similar character leads from the North aisle into what was once a projecting transept. Most of the church, with an attractive side chapel entered by panelled arches, is late Gothic work of the fifteenth and sixteenth centuries. It has a fine Jacobean communion table, and among its monuments is the top half of an effigy, showing a knight in fifteenth-century

A Laudian quartet:

Left **SS. Philip and Jacob,** font and cover (*c.* 1630)

Right **St. Stephen's,** memorial to Martin Pring (d. 1626)

Below left **St. Thomas',** arms of Charles I (1637)

Below right **St. John the Baptist,** communion table (1635)

armour, which must, when complete, have been one of the largest effigies in England. The nave, though it retains its waggon roof, with carved wooden bosses, of a typically West Country character, was much altered in the 1830s when its six-arch arcades were rebuilt, with three arches on each side, to give a better view of the pulpit. Here too are some interesting monuments, and the pulpit and font cover are both splendid examples of seventeenth-century woodwork.

St. Nicholas'[12]

As it is now used, after wartime devastation and some uncertainty over its future, St. Nicholas' is one of the glories of Bristol. The church is another of those built, from the thirteenth century onwards, on a section of the early town wall; the chancel of the medieval church lay over the gateway across the street which led up from Bristol Bridge.

The lower part of the building is a fine rib-vaulted crypt of about 1370, in two aisles and with some richly carved bosses; as in St. John's a crypt, under the full length of the nave, was needed because the slope of the ground meant that the church's main entrance was at the upper level. Some interesting monuments are in the crypt, among them Alderman Whitson's (d. 1627) who founded the Red Maids' School; the crypt now resounds with the busy clatter of a brass rubbing centre.

The upper part of the church, including the fine tower, with its spire, from which the curfew is still sounded at 9 p.m. each day, was built in the Georgian Gothic style and was finished in 1769. Its architect was James Bridges who came from colonial America. This part of the church was gutted by wartime bombing, but it was eventually re-roofed and fitted out by the Bristol Corporation as a splendid museum of local history and church art. It has been described, by the Secretary General of the Arts Council and others, as the finest museum in England of this particular type. A gallery was installed for the upstairs display of local history material, while below it a space, without natural light, is for watercolours and church vestments. The main floor has a magnificent display of local church plate and is dominated, at its East end, by the great altarpiece which Hogarth painted for St. Mary Redcliffe. As the showcases can be moved the space is also available for musical recitals and other cultural events, and as the church was never deconsecrated it is still used for services held by various Christian denominations.

St. Paul's[13]

This church, with its parish taken out of that of St. James, was finished in 1794 as the dominant feature of the fine new enclosure of Portland Square. It was built to serve a residential area, fashionable at first, which grew up on the eastern side of Bristol. The designer was the local architect Daniel Hague. The building is an important Georgian church, and like St. Michael's blends the classical and the Gothic styles. Inside there are

Gothic arches and neo-classical plasterwork along with Doric columns. The steeple, rising high above the surrounding houses, and in its design of stages diminishing in size as they go higher, recalls some of Wren's steeples in London and may also have been inspired by the tower of London's Royal Exchange. But the applied decoration of these stages, and of the tower below them, is unmistakably in the 'Gothick' of the late eighteenth century.

Holy Trinity (St. Philip's)[14] and St. Matthew's (Kingsdown)[15]

These two important churches by Thomas Rickman are in the Perpendicular style which was normal in the early decades of the Gothic Revival. Rickman practised in Birmingham, worked in various styles, and is best known for the naming most widely used for the styles, from Norman to Perpendicular, of English medieval architecture.

Holy Trinity, started in 1829 and opened in 1832, is large and dignified, and one of Rickman's best works. It is now a Caribbean social centre. Aisled, with galleries and large Perpendicular windows, it is of particular note and townscape value for the pair of traceried turrets at its western end.

St. Matthew's, whose simple West tower is a landmark easily seen from many parts of Bristol, was built to serve the new residential area of Cotham and upper Kingsdown. Its galleried interior has been little altered since the church was opened in 1835, and the arms of William IV remind us that this church belongs to the pre-Victorian, pre-ecclesiological phase of the Gothic Revival.

St. George's, Brandon Hill[16]

Built to serve a growing population in the area of Park Street and Berkeley Square, St. George's is Bristol's best Greek Revival church. It was started in 1823, its architect being Sir Robert Smirke who was simultaneously at work on the first part of the British Museum. As the church was built on a steeply sloping site its East end makes a highly dramatic, almost Baroque composition. A four-columned Greek Doric portico stands at the top of a tall flight of steps, and a cupola, like others by Smirke, rises above it. The main entrance to the church, very simply treated, is at the other end as one comes in from Charlotte Street. The interior, well decorated in recent years, is broad and spacious, with galleries resting on slender Greek Doric pillars.

This fine church is still an active centre of worship, and is also the scene of weekly lunchtime concerts, under the auspices of the B.B.C. and the St. George's Music Trust; in this way it is some sort of an equivalent, in Bristol, of London's St. John's, Smith Square.

John Wesley's New Room[17]

This is the oldest building used anywhere for Methodist worship, and in its beautifully restored condition it is among the treasured shrines of Methodism. But John Wesley did not build it as the worshipping place of

A Georgian
pair: Redland
Church and
below John
Wesley's New
Room

Landscaped
steeple: St.
Paul's

a denomination separate from the Church of England. Started in 1739, and much enlarged and improved in 1748, it was a building where Wesley and his early followers, denied the use of the Church of England pulpits in Bristol, could hold services which formed an element in the great movement of religious revival in which they were leaders. Only after John Wesley's death did the 'New Room in the Horsefair' become a chapel of the Methodists as an independent body.

With two entrances, and with fine bronze statues of John and Charles Wesley outside, the building is mostly the structure of 1748. With its gallery, its pulpit, reading desk, and communion table, and with its original mahogany-topped box pews it has a ceiling supported by Roman Doric pillars of stone. In its quiet dignity it is an excellent example of the 'auditory' church interiors made popular by Sir Christopher Wren. Above its ceiling are the rooms, now fitted out as a museum of early Methodism, in which Wesley's preachers stayed when breaking their missionary journeys in Bristol.

Broadmead Baptist Chapel [18]
The congregation whose successors now worship at Broadmead was founded in 1640, the Baptist standpoint being adopted a few years later. The historic chapel was reconstructed in 1695, and was rebuilt and enlarged at various dates between then and 1877. The present chapel, with its pierced concrete tower a striking feature of Bristol's main shopping area, was built, to designs by Ronald Sims, in 1967–69. Its unusual arrangement, with shops at ground-floor level, and the church and halls on the first and second floors, made it possible for this most ancient of Bristol Nonconformist congregations to continue on its historic central site.

Lewin's Mead Unitarian Chapel [19]
Successor to a chapel built about 1662, and later than the Unitarian (originally Independent) churches at Ipswich, Taunton, and Bury St. Edmunds the present building, put up when the Bristol Unitarians were a large and prosperous congregation, is one of England's finest Nonconformist churches of the last years of the eighteenth century. Designed by a London architect, William Blackburn, it was built between 1787 and 1790. It has a restrained, well composed façade of a domestic or secular character, with a plain pediment and an attractive semicircular porch with Ionic columns. The spacious interior, unimpeded by arches or columns, has its original mahogany-topped pews and a pulpit, of delicately worked mahogany, which ranks as one of the most splendid Georgian pulpits anywhere in England.

St. Mary's on the Quay [20]
St. Mary's is another fine neo-classical church, with its six-columned Corinthian portico an important adornment of Colston Avenue at the top end of the Centre. When it was built, the river Frome, with quays on

each side, was still open and accessible to small ships. The church was started by the Catholic Apostolic, or Irvingite, church, but before its completion it was bought by the Roman Catholics, fitted for worship, and opened in 1843. The architect was a local man, Richard Shackleton Pope. It is one of the most central and conspicuous Roman Catholic churches in the very centre of any large English city, and is now served by priests of the Society of Jesus.

The interior, mostly a plain rectangle, with a western gallery but without aisles or arcades, has a most dignified East end. The church has shallow transepts, and the entrance to the sanctuary is flanked by a splendid pair of Corinthian columns.

CENTRAL BRISTOL: SOUTH OF THE AVON

St. Mary Redcliffe[21]

Elizabeth I rightly described this noble building as 'the finest, goodliest, and most famous *parish* church in England'. St. Mary Redcliffe is still this country's finest medieval church which has served nothing but parochial purposes. For many centuries its status was that of a chapel of ease in the large parish of Bedminster; its size and impressiveness came from the urban development, and prosperity, of the northern tip of that parish between the church and Bristol Bridge.

Redcliffe church was first built about the middle of the twelfth century, and the inner North porch, with details in the West wall of the nave and on the inner side of the north-western tower show that by about 1190 it was, for an English parish church of that time, of unusual quality and certainly vaulted. One can, perhaps, compare this building with the splendid vaulted church at New Shoreham in Sussex. But a little over a century later this fine church seemed inadequate. A superb vaulted porch, hexagonal and of great architectural virtuosity and sculptural beauty, was added early in the fourteenth century to the existing North porch. A little later, perhaps about 1340, the complete rebuilding of the church, now planned as a cathedralesque building with double-aisled transepts, a long chancel, a complete system of richly ribbed stone vaults, and the rare feature of an eastern Lady Chapel, was taken in hand. Work seems to have been interrupted by the Black Death, perhaps also by commercial disasters in the Hundred Years' War, but the building was finished about 1400; the tall spire, and the elaborate external decoration of the tower, had been carried out some seventy years earlier. The second bay of the Lady Chapel, with its path under the altar, was added late in the fifteenth century.

As it now stands St. Mary Redcliffe is mostly a church of the Perpendicular Gothic period of English architecture. Its main disadvantage is that the nave and chancel, and still more the transepts, are not quite wide enough for the abbey or cathedral dignity at which the unknown designers aimed. The original spire having largely collapsed in the fifteenth century the top part of the present spire dates from the 1870s. Much of the church's external stonework, particularly the sculptured portions, has had to be replaced in modern restorations.

In addition to the outer North porch fine work of the Decorated period, including 'stellate' ornament round some tomb recesses, and interesting window edging which recalls panelling of about 1335 on window splays in Lichfield Cathedral, occurs in the South aisle of the nave and in the South transept; the aisle vaulting here is unusual in the curvature of some of its ribs. An observant visitor will notice subtle differences, in the chancel, transepts, and nave, in the treatment of such elements as the spaces above the arches, in the tracery of the clerestory windows, and in the design of the vaults. A general feeling of uniformity is belied, in this magnificent, wholly vaulted church, by a careful look at its details. The vault of the nave, and the canopied panels round the large West window, are of particular splendour and the main windows in the transepts, with their traceried transoms, are of great architectural note.

Except for a font of about 1400 which abuts onto a nave pillar the church's medieval fittings have almost wholly disappeared, and the remaining medieval glass, some of it very beautiful, has been grouped in two windows in the base of the tower. A chain-mailed effigy is probably that of a Berkeley, while one in the nave shows a priest in Mass vestments. The best known medieval memorials are those of Chatterton's hero, the eminent Bristol merchant, and later priest, William Canynges the younger, who died in 1474. One effigy shows him, beside his wife, as a layman, while the other, a beautiful work in alabaster, shows him as a priest in choir dress. The double tomb of the Mede family, erected about 1475, is a rare piece of sepulchral design. St. Mary Redcliffe has the best of Bristol's none too numerous brasses; the oldest, a half figure of a civilian of about 1390, was rescued, along with another brass, from the bombed Temple Church. Of the post-Reformation memorials the best known, of great American interest, is the fine mural to Admiral Sir William Penn (d. 1670) the father of William Penn who founded Pennsylvania.

The brass eagle lectern was given in 1638, and the charming marble vase font is of 1755. The finest of the eighteenth-century furnishings are the splendid gates, Baroque ironwork by Edney, first placed at the entrance to the chancel. The pulpit, of 1856, is an excellent achievement of Victorian church woodwork.

St. Thomas'[22]

The first church on this site was dedicated to St. Thomas of Canterbury and was built shortly before 1200. Like St. Mary Redcliffe it was originally a dependent chapel in Bedminster parish. Later in the Middle Ages it had become a large and stately building, with a vaulted North aisle and a north-western tower which, heavily restored, still stands. Late in the eighteenth century the body of the church was pulled down and replaced, between

1789 and 1793, by the present building designed by James Allen. The exterior is plain except for an ornamented East wall, but the late Georgian interior is most dignified with its simple arcades, barrel vault, clerestory windows, and a richly coffered sanctuary ceiling; it was well decorated in 1971–72. Items preserved from the older church include the arms of Charles I, part of the three-decker pulpit, and the notably fine early Georgian reredos and western gallery.

The Temple Church[23]

Though ruined by bombing and never rebuilt Temple church is of great note both for its architectural importance and because its ruins were the first remains of any English *parish* church taken over and repaired by the Ministry of Works (now the Department of the Environment). The Knights Templar were given land in this part of Bedminster parish in the twelfth century, and there are outlines of their oval church, discovered by excavation, inside the shell of the later church built, as the parish church of Holy Cross, after the suppression of the Templars early in the fourteenth century. There is still some early Decorated work in the ruined chancel and its side chapels. The spacious nave, with tall arcades, large windows, and no clerestory, was built in the early Perpendicular style and, as at St. Stephen's, there is a fine Baroque West doorway of the early eighteenth century. The church's most famous feature, and England's best answer to the campanile at Pisa, is the West tower. Started in the 1390s, and a fine piece of Perpendicular Gothic, it seems almost at once to have leant away from an upright position. Its foundations, laid in soft alluvial soil, must have been too weak to carry the weight of new stone-work. Some sixty years later the upper stage was added, but without pinnacles, at an angle slightly less out of the true. The tower survived the bombing, and its bells now hang in Bristol Cathedral.

Zion Chapel (United Reformed)[24]

This chapel, formerly Congregational and built in 1829–30, is well sited near Bedminster Bridge on the south side of the New Cut. A large, dignified building, with a pediment, Greek Doric portico, and Ionic columns to adorn the interior, it was a fine example, before Gothic became fashionable among the Non conformists in Bristol and elsewhere, of the 'tabernacle' type of chapel.

CLIFTON, COTHAM AND REDLAND

Holy Trinity, Hotwells[25]

Built between 1829 and 1830 and designed by C. R. Cockerell this is an important work of the Greek Revival, but it still has features recalling earlier architectural phases. The main exterior composition, on the south side of the church and placed to command the road approach from the top end of the Cumberland Basin, is a deeply recessed and coffered arch

The battle of
the styles:

Grecian: St.
George's,
Brandon Hill
(1823–25) and
below Gothic:
Holy Trinity,
St. Philip's
(1829–32)

A Victorian miscellany:

Left
Bishopsworth,

Right
Stapleton,

Below
Arley Congregational Chapel (now Polish Catholic Church)

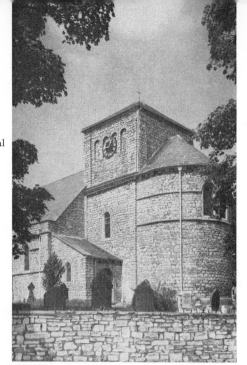

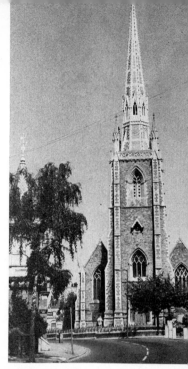

with a sculptured dove at the top and surmounted by an open pediment and a charming bell turret; the whole effect is dramatic in an almost Baroque manner. The original interior, with four pillars supporting a shallow dome, recalled such Wren churches as St. Mary at Hill. Unfortunately the church was gutted by bombing; it has been restored as a single, unimpeded worshipping space.

Christ Church, Clifton[26]

This beautifully sited church, unusually built on a raised podium with grassy slopes on three sides, was at first a chapel of ease in Clifton parish; hence its lack of a churchyard. But since the bombing, without rebuilding, of the parish church of St. Andrew it has become Clifton Parish Church.

Built to serve Clifton Park and the area towards the Downs, Christ Church was started early in 1843 and consecrated in the autumn of 1844. The designer of the original church, with its unaisled nave, transepts, and apsidal chancel, was the local architect Charles Dyer. The splendid tower and spire, whose top is one of the highest and most conspicuous landmarks in Bristol, was by John Norton and dates from 1859, while the aisles, which gave the church a more 'ecclesiological' appearance, were added in the 1880s. Dyer's Early English style, with numerous lancets, was followed throughout, but some trefoil-headed panelling appears on the tower.

All Saints', Clifton[27]

A well known High Church stronghold, and an important example of the substantial replacement of a bombed Victorian church by contrasting work, of a 'contemporary' type, in stone and concrete.

The original church was an important building by G. E. Street, and its chancel was consecrated in 1868. The nave soon followed, and early in the present century a narthex, by G. F. Bodley, was added. The lower part of Street's vaulted tower (now surmounted by a slender spire sheathed with aluminium) still stands, as also do the narthex, now a side chapel, the sacristy, and the church hall. The main fabric, finished in 1967, was designed by Mr. Robert Potter of Salisbury. The main worshipping space is square, with two triangular projections, one containing the baptistry, the other the sanctuary whose high altar lies beneath a modern baldachino moved from the hall which temporarily served as the church. The two walls behind the altar are plain and unwindowed, and the set of single-sloping roofs is so planned that the top lighting of the sanctuary is unseen by the congregation, with the baptistry windows filled by controversial, and to my mind unattractive fibre glass designs by John Piper. The organ pews and choir stalls were newly made for this finely reconstructed church, but many furnishings and fittings were saved from the earlier building.

Clifton Cathedral[28]

The Roman Catholic Cathedral of SS. Peter and Paul is the mother church of a diocese which includes the counties of Avon, Somerset, Gloucestershire and Wiltshire and succeeds the 'Pro' Cathedral, in Park Place, which had been started in 1834, was opened in 1848, and became a cathedral in 1850 when the Clifton diocese was created by Pope Pius IX.

The present building, a new one on a site not formerly occupied by a church, was built between 1970 and 1973. The architects, whose monogram is incised on the building, were the Percy Thomas Partnership. The church serves both as a cathedral (hence its throne and an unusually spacious sanctuary for special ceremonies) and as the parish church for the Catholics in this part of Bristol. It was designed to take account of the liturgical decisions of the second Vatican Council, and must be one of the most up to date Roman Catholic cathedrals in the World. To ensure that all those in the 'nave' can easily see the high altar, and to provide that no one should be too far from it, the architects evolved a plan whose main point was a worshipping space shaped as an elongated hexagon. The sanctuary, another such hexagon, lies to one side of the building, while above it is a lantern tower whose upward-rising members are surmounted, and held in poise, by three vertical members of a 'flèche'. For such a building the only possible material was concrete, of very high quality and mostly poured *in situ*, but with prestressed concrete for small internal pillars and some other items. Most of the exterior is, however, clad with aggregate panels made up of pink Aberdeen granite chips. Concealed top lighting provides nearly all the interior's natural light. One side chapel gives a more secluded space for the reservation of the Blessed Sacrament, private devotion, and weekday Masses.

With its challenging outward aspect, and with a notably impressive interior, Clifton Cathedral is widely recognised as one of England's finest modern churches. A few items, including two bells and important brass tablets outlining the history of the Bishops of Clifton and their predecessors, came from the earlier cathedral. But most of the furnishings and fittings are contemporary and include some good modern works of art. Among them are symbolic windows by Henry Haig, a font of Portland and Purbeck stone by Simon Verity, and the unusual Stations of the Cross, concrete sculpture by William Mitchell. The doors, with a sculptural coating of fibreglass by William Mitchell were, like those of the new Catholic Cathedral at Liverpool, given by the local municipality.

Buckingham Baptist Chapel[29]

Opened in 1847 and designed by R. S. Pope this chapel was, in its own time and in contrast with the 'Regency' character of the neighbouring Buckingham Place, unusual among Bristol's Nonconformist churches in being built in a version of the French Gothic of the late thirteenth century. It has large 'Geometrical' side windows, and a striking façade with three doorways, a wheel window, tall pinnacles, and panelling. The French Gothic precedent was followed in Clifton Down Congregational Chapel,[30] designed by the Roman Catholic architect Charles Hansom and opened

A Baptist trio:

Left

Horfield Baptist
Church

Right

Kensington
Chapel,
Stapleton Road

Below

Broadmead
Baptist Chapel

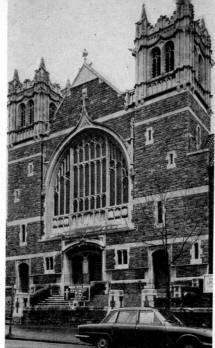

in 1868; the tower and spire intended for this striking apsidal building were never put up.

St. Mary's, Cotham[31]

Now used as an Anglican church, this building was completed in 1843 as the Highbury Congregational Chapel. It is of considerable architectural and historic interest. In the Perpendicular style, and with aisles, arcades, and a low clerestory, it was a much more 'churchlike' building than most of those so far used by the Nonconformists. It was the first church by the important Victorian architect William Butterfield who from then onwards strictly, and as a matter of conscience, confined himself to work for the Established Church. The Highbury commission had come to the young architect because the wife of the second H. O. Wills, of the tobacco family and a devoted Congregationalist, was his aunt. In 1863 the talented Bristol architect E. W. Godwin added an apse (later lengthened) and a tower in the manner of that at New College, Oxford.

A corbel at the end of an arcade was carved, by Eric Gill, into an attractive memorial to Dr. Arnold Thomas, one of Highbury's Ministers, who died in 1924.

The church now replaces two Anglican churches, not far away, which were declared redundant; the shade of Butterfield must rejoice at the change.

Redland Church[32]

This is a notably attractive building of the eighteenth century. It was originally built, between 1740 and 1743, as a private chapel for a family living inconveniently far from their parish church at Westbury-on-Trym, by John Cossins and his wife Martha of Redland Court. It was not consecrated till the 1750s, and only became a full parish church in 1942. Though its initial designs may have been by John Strahan, the architect of Cossins' mansion, it was finished under the supervision of William Halfpenny who designed the Coopers' Hall in King Street.

The church is small and rectangular, unaisled and with a short projecting sanctuary. Its main exterior feature is its western façade, with a fine niche above a segmentally headed doorway, four Ionic pilasters supporting a pediment, and a striking bell turret, octagonal with an ornamental urn at each corner, and capped by a leaded cupola. There is no East window, but a rusticated blind arch on the East wall has corbels in the form of negroes' heads.

As the tower stands directly over the chapel's West end its design allows for an entrance vestibule, a western gallery, and a fine composition of arches and balustrading. There are busts of John and Martha Cossins by Rysbrack, and two other busts probably by the same sculptor. Other carving, in stone and wood, is by the Bristolian Thomas Paty. This is notably fine in the sanctuary, where a richly coffered ceiling, and a row of winged cherubs' heads, rise above the panelling and the rich limewood

Clifton
Cathedral:
the First
Station of the
Cross
and exterior

carving which frames the side panels and the central picture, a copy by Vanderbank of Annibale Caracci's *Embalming of Christ*. The pulpit is also a fine work of the eighteenth century, and the communion table is a rare achievement of the same time, being supported by a gilt eagle with spread wings and two brackets which combine cabriole legs and female torsos. The ornate vase font is another work by Thomas Paty.

SOME 'VILLAGE' CHURCHES

Westbury on Trym[33]
This fine church, long that of a College of secular canons, is of the utmost historic and architectural interest. Its origins, earlier than those of any church in the centre of Bristol, go back to at least the first decade of the ninth century. For twelve years, from 962, an important Benedictine community (which moved to Ramsey) was at Westbury and the monastery was later dependent on the cathedral priory at Worcester. From the 1190s the church remained collegiate.

None of Westbury church dates from the pre-Conquest or Norman period of its history. The nave, with tall arcades, and the South aisle which has some Early English lancets and fine sedilia of the thirteenth century, date from soon after 1200. Most of the rest of the church, of various dates, is Perpendicular work. The western tower, whose pinnacles were renewed in a Victorian restoration, and the nave clerestory with its eastern window a typically Gloucestershire feature, are of the fifteenth century. The choir, with the rare feature, in England, of a late Gothic apse, and its large southern chapel are excellent Perpendicular work, being part of the additions made by Bishop Carpenter of Worcester (1443-76) who augmented the college's revenues and hoped to make Westbury church a second cathedral in his diocese. His tomb, rebuilt in 1853 by Oriel College, Oxford of which he had been Provost, is in the choir. Later memorials commemorate prominent residents in the parish.

The quadrangular buildings of the college are some distance from the church, down by the river Trym on a site which accommodated the earlier monastery. They were built, in their final medieval form, by Bishop Carpenter and resembled those of some small Oxford colleges. The best remaining features are the gate tower with its finely vaulted passageway, and two of the rounded corner turrets with their attractive caps of a concave silhouette.

Henbury[34]
As at Westbury the history of the manor here takes us far back into the Anglo-Saxon period. An estate there was given to the bishopric of Worcester in 692, and all through the Middle Ages the manor at Henbury was an important episcopal residence. The church and its churchyard have well kept the atmosphere of a country parish. The oldest parts of the present building are the nave and the simple western tower, both Early

Three contemporary churches:

Right Lockleaze,

Below left St. Bernadette's, Wells Road and

Below right Christ the Servant, Stockwood

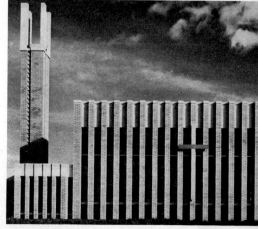

English and with a low clerestory and other features of about 1300. The tall arcades, each of six arches with round pillars, are notable work; so too are the North and South doorways whose heads are segmental, not semicircular or pointed. Other details include good early Gothic capitals and continuously moulded arches like those of the Wells school.

The church has fine Baroque monuments to the Southwells of Kingsweston, and to other well-to-do families resident in the parish. But Henbury's best known memorial is the churchyard grave, with its two headstones, to Scipio Africanus, the negro page boy of the Earl of Suffolk and Bindon (not Bradon as in the inscription) who died in 1720.

Stapleton[35]
One of Bristol's best Victorian churches and the successor, in 1854–57, to an older and much smaller village church which had a low Perpendicular West tower. The present building is finely sited at the top of a gentle hill, and most of it was built, at his own expense, by Bishop Monk, the first holder of the combined Gloucester and Bristol bishopric, who turned the nearby Stapleton House (now Colston's School) into his palace. Designed by John Norton and with rich sculptural decoration, the church is a typical 'ecclesiological' building in the Decorated style. Its nave, without a clerestory, has five bays, and the church has a fine, commanding West tower with a graceful spire. A square font of about 1200 and several mural monuments survive from the old church.

Brislington[36]
This is another village church, once in Somerset, and pleasantly situated on a hill slope so that its beautiful tower dominates the village below it. A fine churchyard cross remains near the porch. Most of the fabric is of the Perpendicular period, the nave being without a clerestory and with a North aisle of the early decades of last century. The southern arcade is typical West of England work of the fifteenth century, and part of the arch which divides the South chapel from the chancel is panelled underneath in the manner of many Somerset churches.

The church's best feature is its West tower, of local pennant stone with ornamental details in freestone. At its south-eastern corner the stair turret is capped, in the local manner, by a tall pinnacle rising above the others. The panelled battlements have the rare feature, in the middle of each side, of a canopied niche; they all contain their original figures, one of them a Trinity group.

Bishopsworth[37]
The successor of a medieval chapel, destroyed at the Reformation, in this southern expanse of Bedminster parish, Bishopsworth church was designed by the Bristol architect S. C. Fripp and was built in 1842–43. Said to be modelled on a church in Caen it is a fine example of the neo-Norman style which had, in the 1840s, a brief spell of popularity. The nave has an

34

St. Augustine's
Whitchurch:
an interior
view

Highbury
Chapel (now
St. Mary's,
Cotham):
memorial to
Arnold
Thomas by
Eric Gill

IN·MEMORY·OF
THE·REVEREND
HENRY·ARNOLD·THOMAS
M·A·LL·D·
THE·BELOVED·PASTOR·OF
THIS·CHURCH·FOR·47·YRS
BORN·13·JUNE·1848·
DIED·28·JUNE·1924·
Great grace was upon him.

aisle, there are no transepts, and a short apsidal sanctuary lies east of the low tower over the chancel.

OTHER OUTLYING CHURCHES

A short booklet, with its main emphasis on historic interest, and on the architectural and townscape value of the churches mentioned, can only include a proportion of Bristol's churches of various denominations. I am well aware of many churches which I cannot describe, still less would I wish to disregard them as active centres of worship and spiritual life. Of these, however, a number demand *some* reference for their architectural interest and as visual elements in the Bristol scene. Many others of architectural importance were bombed in the war or have since been pulled down or disused for worship. These, in particular, included some Nonconformist chapels of considerable merit, also some Victorian buildings consecrated for Anglican use. Those which are now briefly mentioned all stand and are still used for worship.

East of central Bristol, and beyond the St. Paul's area, the church of *St. Agnes*,[38] was built as the central element in the Clifton College Mission. The church, by W. Wood Bethell, was consecrated in 1886 and its fine tower, with a spirelet rising, in the Bristol manner, high above its north-western stairway turret, was finished in the next year. In the Decorated style, and with a clerestory above the tall cylindrical pillars and arches of its nave arcades, St. Agnes' is one of Bristol's more imposing Victorian churches. Not far away the *Parkway Methodist church*[39] results from the merging of two Methodist congregations in this part of Bristol. Built in 1970–71 it is octagonal, with a spirelet set pleasantly above its high-rising roof; the church also has some striking modern glass on a symbolic pattern. The architect was Eustace Button of Bristol.

In Stapleton Road an excellent Grecian façade, with two Corinthian columns, at first-floor level, below a pediment, is that of the *Kensington Baptist Church*[40]. Succeeding an earlier chapel on a different site this chapel was built in 1886–88 and was designed by the Glasgow architect T. I. Watson. In its correct Grecianism it looks earlier than its date and has one of Bristol's most handsome Nonconformist façades. Further out in the same direction the early Victorian Gothic *St. Simon's*[41] was built, in 1846–47, to designs by S. B. Gabriel. 'Ecclesiological' in the late thirteenth-century manner it has a northern tower and a good broach spire. It has recently become the Greek Orthodox church of SS. Peter and Paul.

St. Werburgh's,[42] at the top of Mina Road, is interesting as the partial rebuilding, on a new site, of the church once in Corn Street in the city centre. The tower, most beautiful with a fan-vaulted tower space, panelled upper stages, and traceried battlements, was originally built before 1480 and was faithfully re-erected. The body of the church, with a three-gabled East end and a projecting sanctuary, is less exact as a copy of the old St. Werburgh's which was rebuilt in the Georgian Gothic of the

1760s; it may represent the Victorian architect Bevan's idea of how the church looked before that rebuilding. Some monuments, including the fine Renaissance tomb of Alderman Barker (d. 1607) who had been Mayor of Bristol, were moved from the old building, and the church also has a simple iron sword rest of the eighteenth century.

Near the railway line (laid down after the building of the church) at Stapleton Road station *St. Mark's, Easton*[43] is a most convincing example of the neo-Norman style whose popularity covered the 1840s. Designed by the versatile Charles Dyer and completed, after his death, by S. B. Gabriel it has an apsidal chancel and, on its northern side, an arcaded and boldly capped tower with sculptured animals climbing gaily on its cap. Not far away, and also close to the railway. *All Hallows', Easton*[44] is, even in its incomplete state, a handsome and ambitious church in the Decorated style. By Oatley and Lawrence and consecrated in 1901 the church has an apsidal chancel with a fine arcade and a narrow ambulatory (now a vestry) behind the high altar. Each of the twin-gabled transepts has an arcade of two stately arches. Only three bays of the nave were finished, but an attractive western termination was eventually built to Sir George Oatley's designs. The church hall, finished in 1913, is another excellent building, by Oatley, from the time when he was making his designs for the University.

Along Whitehall Road the large church of *St. Ambrose*[45], in this case fully completed, was, like All Hallows', established with help from one of the vestries of a central parish. Sometimes known as 'the cathedral of East Bristol', it is a spacious building by the Bristol architects W. V. and A. R. Gough. Early Perpendicular in style, with some touches of Arts and Crafts Gothic, it has a clerestoried chancel, a spacious seven-bay nave, East and West windows of seven lights, an imposing southern tower, and a fanciful leaded cupola over the chancel arch.

Out on the road to Gloucester and Cheltenham the *Arley Congregational Chapel*[46] (now the Polish Catholic church of Our Lady of Ostrobrama) is extremely well sited at the fork of two roads. Its narrow end makes a striking composition in which a clock tower of Renaissance character rises above a curved Corinthian portico. The chapel was built in 1854–55 with John Foster as its architect. Further up, on a commanding slope East of the main road the steeple of the Gothic *David Thomas Memorial Church*[47] (United Reformed) is a graceful townscape element. By Stuart Colman and with a broach spire over an octagonal stage it recalls the even more graceful steeple which Colman designed for a Congregational chapel, now demolished, in Sneyd Park. The David Thomas church was built in 1879–81. Higher up Gloucester Road, and directly facing it, the broad façade of *Horfield Baptist church*[48], with its two low flanking towers and a great Perpendicular West window of twelve lights, is a striking Arts and Crafts Gothic achievement and makes a fine contribution to the local scene. By the Bristol architect R. Milverton Drake it was started in 1900.

At the bottom of Whiteladies Road the *Victoria Methodist church*[49], by the Bristol partners John Foster and Joseph Wood and opened in 1863, is a high Gothic contrast to its classical neighbours the Victoria Rooms and the Royal West of England Academy. Above its roof it has a French Gothic flèche and its delicate polychrome contrast was well revealed by recent cleaning. In Westbury Park the fine stone-built church of *St. Alban*[50], of 1907–13 and by the Bristol architect C. F. W. Dening, is Perpendicular and transeptal with narrow passageway aisles on each side of its chancel. Its effect is diminished by the lack of a tower, but it is one of Bristol's best early twentieth century churches.

Two churches worth noticing in Bristol's north-western outskirts are of later dates. One, by Sir George Oatley and opened in 1928, is *St. Edyth's, Seamills*[51], cruciform with an embattled central tower and with most of its stylistic points looking to the thirteenth century; the nave has never been finished. Red pennant and Bath stone are well contrasted in the exterior. *Shirehampton church*[52], by P. Hartland Thomas, a Bristol architect who did distinctive work between the wars, is of about the same date. It has a striking bell cote with an angular silhouette, while in the body of the church Jacobean Perpendicular is used in a characterful way. Another church by Hartland Thomas is *St. Oswald's, Bedminster Down*[53], finished in 1929 in a late Gothic blend of brownish purple pennant and Bath stone, with a pointed tunnel vault across the nave. The stocky western tower has an almost Norman silhouette.

Many churches, of various denominations, have been finished in Bristol since 1945; I here give a small selection of the more recent buildings, in outlying areas, which have some architectural distinction.

The Anglican church at *Lockleaze*[54], by T. H. B. Burrough, was opened in 1956, being built of prefabricated concrete units of types also used for chimney stacks and other industrial buildings; a graceful belfry is made up of thin concrete struts. The nave is octagonal, with a sanctuary and an upper Lady Chapel in a projecting limb. The church has a concrete figure of Christ by Ernest Pascoe and beautiful coloured glass by Margaret Trehearne. At Lawrence Weston *St. Peter's church*[55] replaces an earlier post-war building. By J. Ralph Edwards and finished in 1961 it is rectangular with the east-west dimension less than the breadth. It has a thin concrete tower, sensitively patterned brickwork, and good *dalle de verre* windows by Pierre Fourmaintreux.

In southern Bristol the best known recent church, a striking introduction to the city as one comes in by the Wells road, is *St. Bernadette's*[56], a Roman Catholic building finished in 1968 and designed by James Leask of the Bristol architects Kenneth Nealon, Tanner, and Partners. A double hyperbolic paraboloid roof and brick curtain walls enclose a square interior arranged diamondwise; the motif of a square is used for the brick font and many other furnishings. At Stockwood, the church of *Christ the Servant*[57] and its hall were started by J. Ralph Edwards, the first part being finished in 1964, and completed in 1971 to designs, sympathetic to the earlier work, by John Maggs. The main worshipping space is nearly

39

square, with a side chapel and glass by Fourmaintreux, while the exterior has a striking alternation of slender brick uprights and narrow windows. A thin tower of grey brick has corner pinnacles of granite aggregate. By an ecumenical adjustment of service times the Roman Catholic priests of St. Bernadette's say Mass here twice each Sunday.

Ecumenism also appears, in another direction, in *St. Augustine's Anglican and Methodist Church Centre*[58] near Whitchurch.* By the Bristol architects Moxley, Jenner and Partners, and with attractive yellowish brown brickwork the church, entered through a walled garden, has a single-slope roof and a thin belfry made of four brick uprights. Inside, a figure of the crucified Christ is by Ernest Pascoe. Money for the building came from the sale of the site of the medieval *St. Augustine's the Less* in College Green; an old bell and Communion plate have come from that church. The early Norman tub font (the oldest in Bristol) and its Jacobean cover were brought from the Somerset church of East Lydford.

---

* The old village and medieval church of Whitchurch lie beyond the city boundary, and are thus outside this book's scope.

Acknowledgements

The photographs in this book are reproduced by permission of the following (references are to page numbers):

Administrator, Clifton Cathedral: 31(top)

Cedric Barker: 26(bottom), 29(top left)

T. H. B. Burrough: 33(top)

City of Bristol Publicity Dept.: 4(bottom), 19(bottom)

Gordon Kelsey: 7(bottom), 16, 36

John Laing & Son Ltd.: 29(bottom)

John K. Maggs: 33(bottom right)

Moxley, Jenner & Ptnrs.: 35

John Trelawney-Ross: cover, 4(top), 5, 7(top), 8, 11, 12, 19(top), 20, 25, 26(top), 29(top right)

Percy Thomas Partnership & John Laing: 31(bottom)

The street map is by courtesy of Geographers' A-Z Map Company Ltd. of Sevenoaks, Kent.